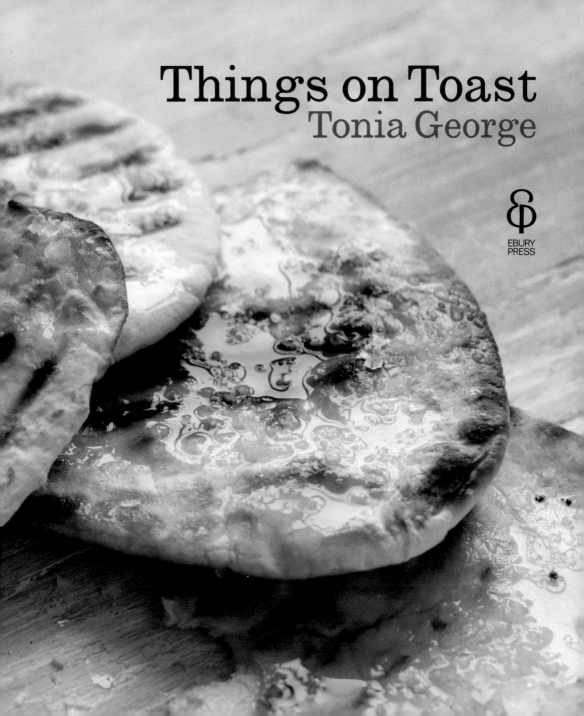

Things on Toast
Tonia George

EBURY
PRESS

To my mum, who always found time
to make me toast in the morning!

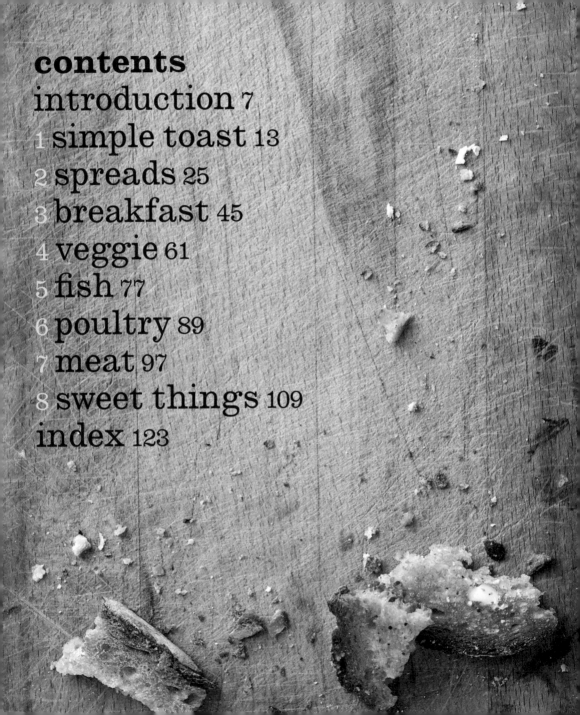

contents

introduction

I could live on toast. I wouldn't need an imaginary desert island to force me to make that choice; it's quite simply one of the most perfect foods ever invented. For what satisfies hunger better – or quicker – than a simple golden slab of toast dripping with butter? What stirs up the appetite better than wafts of yeasty bread slowly caramelising? This promise, the sublime smell, is often just as tantalising as the first bite. This book is dedicated to the enjoyment of toast in the most indulgent manner: showering the bed with crumbs and not caring that they are going to tickle you for days after.

But to truly celebrate toast in all its crisp, fluffy, charred glory, we need to liberate it from the breakfast table; release it from the shackles of the toast rack. After all, I eat toast throughout the day, most days of the year. Griddled sourdough draped with tomatoes and drizzled with grassy olive oil with a glass of Chianti makes a wonderful start to a summer's evening, in the same way that a midnight snack of chocolate spread on hot white toast will ease you into a wintry night of sweet dreams.

I have always shunned the conformists' 'meat and two veg' rule in favour of something altogether more relaxed. I get a smug glow when I settle down to a supper of soft-boiled eggs with soldiers slathered in Gentleman's Relish and a green salad. It reminds me just how good it is to be an adult – even if that only really means having the choice to behave like a child again.

Toast has never been a friend of restraint. It needs to be generously smothered with butter or unctuous juices to save it from being dry. Dry toast is purely for when you're sick; a good comforter. What you're after is juices dripping into every pore of the crisp surface, whether from the oily flesh of an avocado, or the rosy juices of a rare steak. As John Thorne wrote in *Pot on the Fire* (2000), 'Unbuttered toast is a substance half complete, and to be forced to eat it in that state is necessarily to feel deprived.' I don't advocate deprivation, especially when it comes to toast.

Toast is much more versatile than many people give it credit for. It goes way beyond the ubiquitous cheese or beans on toast (although you will find splendid versions of both these masterpieces on the pages that follow). Toasting bread transforms bread into a crisp counterfoil that is a perfect companion to almost anything, whether that is a spoonful of voluptuous lemon curd, some softly scrambled eggs or a tangle of watercress and flaky mackerel. It is equally as happy to play the supporting role to slices of pork with a punchy salsa verde, as it is stepping into the lead, to become an edible scoop for different pâtés and dips.

My only rule is that any jams, butters or homemade toppings (such as my Chocolate Hazelnut Spread (see page 30)) need to come to room temperature before they meet the hot toast, so the heat of the toast can turn them into molten pools of deliciousness. I keep a small chunk of butter at room temperature so I don't have to battle with butter from the fridge and don't have to acknowledge the existence of margarine.

Whatever country you are in, there is always a toast recipe to match and they often have one common factor: they are thrifty ways of reviving bread that has seen better days. Stale bread was endemic in rural peasant life, since fresh bread was not available every day and wastage couldn't be tolerated. Born out of this are French *tartines*, Italian crostini and bruschette, Spanish *pintxos* and the various manifestations of bread dipped in egg – eggy bread, *pain perdu*, *torrijas* or French toast, depending on where you are in the world and how you like to describe it.

Precisely why toasting became and has remained 'so peculiarly English a delicacy', aside from the thrift issue, is suggested by Elizabeth David in the final pages of her tome *English Bread and Yeast Cookery*: 'I wonder if our open fires and coal ranges were not more responsible than the high incidence of stale bread for the popularity of toast', she muses after having seen a multitude of Victorian toasting tools in cookbooks and museums.

Many people wax lyrical about their nostalgic memories of toasting bread over open fires. The smoke does indeed add a wonderful flavour and ensures the toast remains fluffy inside and charred on the out, but it is no longer an everyday option. Once again, Elizabeth David puts it so astutely when she cynically recalls that, 'more toast fell off the fork into the fire and was irretrievably blackened than ever reached our plates'. If you are toasting over a campfire or barbecue, forget the toasting fork and try to procure the sort of clamp usually reserved for incarcerating fish. If you're an Aga owner, you'll be able to use this on your hot plate too. My favoured method for toast is a cast-iron griddle; it doesn't compete with the electric toaster on convenience and speed, but it gives you attractive dark lines and a more char-grilled flavour. Be brave and toast it right up until the moment you think it is burnt; after all, the word toast comes from the Latin *tostum*, meaning 'to scorch'. The grill is useful when you want to melt the topping, when making Welsh rabbit or a hot goats' cheese salad. Always toast the bread a little before you add the topping and spread the topping right to the edges so the crusts don't get too singed.

I think the success of toast relies largely on choosing a good-quality bread in the first instance; one with a low water content, or it will steam and go soft the minute it hits the plate. Second, it must be cut correctly. Toast cut into triangles tastes far superior to toast cut into squares, I'm sure of it. Don't ask me to explain the hows or whys, but the same principle applies

when slicing bread; it needs to be at least 1–2 cm thick to achieve that softness inside without becoming brittle (which is only acceptable for Melba toast).

When choosing your bread, you have to think about the suitability of the flavour as well as the texture, so it can do its job properly. French toast needs a light, fluffy bread, such as *challah*, whereas bruschette require a dense rustic bread. The term 'rustic' is a very loose definition for any bread with a nutty, wholesome flavour and an uneven holey texture, such as a *pugliese* or *pain de campagne*. The infamous inimitable *Poilâne* sourdough represents a further step in this direction; the nuttiness being joined by a sour tang. These rustic breads are quite stubborn about toasting compared to the more compliant white bloomer, but they have a deeper flavour and make great bruschette or sturdy bases for heartier toppings such as a char-grilled steak.

Having noisily crunched my way through my whole body weight in toast, I can truly say there is no food as versatile, thrifty and mightily delicious as the humble piece of toast. I always knew I could live on toast, but I think anyone could live on toast and never tire of it. It is indeed the best thing since sliced bread.

Note: All eggs are medium unless specified otherwise. Over temperatures are based on conventional ovens; for fan ovens, reduce the temperature by 20°C.

simple toast

Grilled buttered toast
Melba toast
Olive oil and rosemary bruschetta
Pan con tomate
Garlic and thyme pitta toasts
Crostini
Cinnamon butter toast

grilled buttered toast

Buttering toast on one side before grilling adds a very different character to toast. Not only does the butter become nutty, it softens the bread. You do need to cut off the crusts, as they will burn before the middle is golden.

makes 4
4 slices white bread, crusts removed
Softened butter, for spreading

▸ Position the shelf under the grill about 10 cm away from the element and preheat the grill to high. Find yourself a baking sheet. Once the grill is red hot, slide the bread on to the sheet and grill for 3 minutes until it is nicely golden.

▸ Flip the bread over on the other side and spread the untoasted side with the butter. Grill for another 2–3 minutes, watching it like a hawk until the butter starts to smell nutty and look golden. Slide off the bread on to a chopping board. Cut into triangles.

melba toast

Melba toast was invented after Escoffier overheard Madame Ritz bemoaning the thickness of toast. He immediately set his mind to creating a thinner toast to please his boss's wife. However, it was actually named after opera singer Dame Nellie Melba, who became ill and took to eating slivers of toast as part of her invalid diet.

makes 16
4 x 1 cm-thick slices white bread

▸ Position the shelf under the grill about 15 cm away from the element and preheat the grill to high. Place the bread on a baking sheet and grill on both sides until quite golden. Remove from the grill.

▸ Using a large, sharp knife, slice off the crusts, then with one palm on top of the toast, slice horizontally through the bread to split into two thin halves. Cut each one into four triangles and place back on the baking sheet and under the grill for 1–2 minutes until brittle and curling at the edges.

olive oil and rosemary bruschetta

A bruschetta is a large piece of toast, topped with ingredients. You can also make a simple one flavoured with herbs and garlic. The bread should resemble typical *pugliese* bread; a rustic bread with a nutty flavour and an open texture, which will give you an abrasive surface to rub the garlic against. Any sourdough works well. It is best made over an open fire or barbecue or, failing that, a ridged griddle pan, to give it that charred exterior and chewy inside. The golden rule is to rub the rough surface with the garlic while it is still warm so it absorbs deep into the pores of the toast.

makes 8

8 slices country bread or *pain rustique*
2 garlic cloves, peeled and halved
1 sprig rosemary
4 tbsp extra virgin olive oil
Salt and freshly ground black pepper

▸ Place a griddle pan over a high flame or light a barbecue well in advance. Once the griddle pan is smoking hot, or the barbecue's coals are glowing an ashen grey, pop the bread on and toast for 2–3 minutes on each side until charred in places and crisp all over. Turn over and cook until the other side matches.

▸ Take off the heat and rub with the cut side of the garlic cloves while still warm and press the sprig of rosemary against the surface of the bread, rubbing it to release its flavour. Drizzle with the olive oil and season. Eat immediately or the bread slices will become too soggy.

pan con tomate

The difference between this Spanish toast and the previous Italian bruschetta recipe is that the tomato is really squashed against the bread to make it soften. If over-ripe tomatoes are around, so much the better. Its flavour is tickled out by a scattering of crunchy sea salt. Get the bread quite charred, as the juices from the tomatoes and the slug of olive oil will soften any harshness; a trick left over from the days of thrifty peasant food, no doubt. Use ripe tomatoes at the temperature they would be if plucked straight off their vines.

makes 6

6 slices rustic bread
5 tbsp extra virgin olive oil
2 garlic cloves, peeled and halved
2 large, over-ripe juicy tomatoes
Sea salt flakes

► Heat the barbecue well in advance, or use a griddle pan if inside and heat that on a high heat until really hot. Place the bread, cut side up, on the barbecue or griddle pan to lightly toast one side, which should take about a minute. Turn over and press the other side down on to the griddle, or just leave it to do its thing on a barbecue for 2 minutes until lightly scored and charred.

► While hot, rub each slice with the cut side of a garlic clove, then the cut side of a tomato, really pushing all the seeds into the surface. Lay the toasts on a platter and drizzle with the olive oil and scatter with salt. Serve with some plates of cured Spanish sausage and ham.

garlic and thyme pitta toasts

This is a good trick for making pitta breads stretch further. It is perfect for serving at drinks parties, as everyone thinks you have bought really special bread. I like to serve these with fried halloumi cheese, or a bean dip such as the one on page 37.

makes 25

4 tbsp extra virgin olive oil
1 tsp chilli flakes
1 tsp dried thyme leaves
1 garlic clove, peeled and crushed
5 pitta breads, split open

▸ Position the shelf under the grill about 15 cm away from the element and preheat the grill to high. Mix the olive oil with the chilli, thyme and garlic.

▸ Brush the pitta breads on their cut side with the flavoured oil and lay on a baking sheet, oil-side down. Grill for 2–3 minutes until crisp on one side. Remove from the grill and turn over. Grill for 3–4 minutes on the other side until crisp, but don't allow the crushed garlic to become too dark. Break up into pieces or cut into strips.

crostini

Crostini is a Tuscan invention, made with their ubiquitous salt-free bread, *pan sciocco* (silly bread). To balance this lack of salt, the toppings are generally quite salty, from anchovies and cured salamis to those with capers and Parmesan. The ciabatta crostini are a little more substantial than the canapé crostini and work well as a base for any antipasti. They can be topped with a homemade dip or some cured meat, cheese, sardines – almost anything. I make the canapé crostini for parties where you really only want a very small bite that you can eat without a plate. I bake them in the oven and they dry out more than they would if grilled – they can then be kept in an airtight container for up to a week.

ciabatta crostini

makes 8
1 *ciabatta*
5 tbsp extra virgin olive oil

▸ Slice the *ciabatta* 2 cm thick and place on a flat baking sheet. Position the shelf under the grill approximately 10–15 cm away from the element and preheat the grill to high.

▸ Toast the *ciabatta* for 2–3 minutes on each side. Remove from the oven and brush with olive oil while still warm.

canapé crostini

makes 15
1 x 25 cm *baguette*
5 tbsp extra virgin olive oil

▸ Preheat the oven to 200°C/Gas 6. Cut the *baguette* into 1.5 cm thick slices and place Brush one side lightly with the oil and bake in the oven for 12–15 minutes until crisp.

▸ Top with whatever topping you like, or bundle into an airtight container.

cinnamon butter toast

The smell of this toast is sweet, spicy and heavenly. It is ideal for moments when there is nothing to snack on, because you inevitably have these four ingredients tucked away. You can always make it with caster sugar if you don't have any soft brown. I sometimes add a dash of rosewater to the sugar before spreading it on the toast, for a more exotic, slightly Moroccan-inspired flavour. If you can resist making a hot chocolate to go alongside, then I congratulate you.

makes 6

1 tbsp ground cinnamon
4 tbsp light muscavado sugar
30 g unsalted butter
a drop of rosewater (optional)
6 slices white bread

▸ Position the shelf under the grill approximately 10–15 cm away from the element and preheat the grill to high. Mix together the cinnamon, sugar and butter in a bowl and set aside.

▸ Spread the cinnamon sugar over both sides of the toast and place on a baking sheet. Slide under the hot grill for 1–2 minutes on each side until bubbling and golden. Cut into triangles and serve.

2

spreads

Quick lemon curd
Quick apricot jam
Vanilla and thyme honey
Chocolate hazelnut spread
Whipped blackberry soft cheese
Pecan maple and lemon butter
Orange blossom honey butter
Gentleman's relish
White beans, chorizo and rocket
Avocado, lime and black pepper
Creamed Parmesan
Smoked mackerel pâté
Artichokes and Parma ham

quick lemon curd

When I was taught to make lemon curd I was told to stand over a bain-marie for what seemed like hours, laboriously stirring until I felt the egg thicken. It was a revelation when I discovered in Stephanie Alexander's book, *The Cook's Companion*, that the acidity in the lemons and amount of sugar stop any curdling and it can all be made in less than 5 minutes.

makes 300 ml jar
100 g unsalted butter
200 g golden caster sugar
Zest and juice of 3 medium
   or 2 large unwaxed lemons
3 eggs, beaten

▸ Sterilise your jar, by running the jar and lid through the dishwasher, or boil in hot water for a couple of minutes and then invert on to a kitchen towel to dry.

▸ Put the butter, sugar and lemon zest and juice into a heavy-based saucepan. Turn a hob ring to low and melt the contents of the pan, stirring until blended. Remove the pan from the heat and strain in the eggs to remove the lumpy bits.

▸ Slide the pan back on to the heat and stir and scrape the bottom of the pan for 5–10 minutes, until the mixture thickens and looks like curd. Don't be tempted to turn up the heat or it will scramble the eggs. The curd will cool and set further on cooling. Spoon into a sterilised jar (see above).

▸ For lemon curd, you need a white fluffy bloomer. Slice it thickly and toast in the toaster. Butter while hot and spread on a thick dollop of lemon curd. The lemon curd will keep for four weeks in the fridge.

quick apricot jam

The secret to good apricot jam is hidden deep inside their stones. It is, of course, the apricot kernels. These small nuts exude an almondy fragrant perfume, which gives jam an ambrosial flavour. Bashing the stones is a knack; if you do it too gently, the whole stone goes flying across the room; too enthusiastically, and you will shatter the kernel inside. Luckily, you only need a few kernels, so you get plenty of practice. Choose unripe apricots as the pectin levels are higher.

makes 4 x 250 ml jars
750 g (about 15) apricots,
    halved and stoned
Juice of 1 lemon
750 g granulated sugar

▸ Pop two or three saucers in the fridge and sterilise your jam jars (see page 26).

▸ Put a few apricot stones in a freezer bag and whack each one with a rolling pin to break the stones. Inside the stones you will find white, much softer kernels. Pick out six of the most intact kernels and discard the others.

▸ Pop the apricots and kernels in a large, non-reactive stainless steel saucepan with 200 ml of water and the lemon juice and bring to the boil. Cook for 20 minutes, until collapsed then add the sugar. Cook over a low heat until dissolved.

▸ Turn up the heat and boil for about 15 minutes, until a sugar thermometer reaches 105°C. You will see the bubbles change from small to large. To check, put half a teaspoon of jam on to one of the chilled saucers, return it to the freezer for 30 seconds, then prod the top. A skin will form when the jam is set. If not, keep going and try again in another 2–5 minutes.

▸ Leave for 10 minutes to cool a little, then spoon into the sterilised jars, cover with waxed discs and lids while still warm, label and date. Store in a cool, dark place for up to 6 months. Spread onto hot toasted brioche to serve.

vanilla and thyme honey

Once you get the basic premise of flavouring honey, you can play around with lots of different aromatics. Try adding warm spices such as cloves, cinnamon sticks or orange peel for a Christmassy feel, and lavender in the summer. They make a really thoughtful gift and take no time at all.

makes 2 x 250 ml jars
2 sprigs thyme, washed and dried
1 vanilla pod, split lengthways
500 g clear honey

▶ Place all the ingredients in a small saucepan over a gentle heat. Bring to a gentle boil and then turn off the heat. While still warm, pour into the sterilised jars (see page 26), making sure each one gets a sprig of thyme, cover with a disc of plastic or a lid and leave at room temperature to infuse for a week before using, to allow the flavours to develop. Drizzle across any hot toast or toasted muffins.

chocolate hazelnut spread

Anyone that was addicted to Nutella as a child will love this home-made version. It has just the right texture to remain firm, like a truffle in a jar, but show it some hot toast and it will graciously melt into every pore.

makes 2 x 250 ml jars
50 g toasted blanched hazelnuts
200 g plain chocolate
2 tbsp caster sugar
250 ml double cream
100 g unsalted butter

► Preheat the oven to 200°C/Gas 6 and sterilise the glass jars (see page 26). Find a heatproof bowl that will sit on top of a saucepan. Fill the pan with water so it is about one-third full and bring to the boil. Turn down the heat to so it is barely simmering.

► Meanwhile, place the nuts in a roasting tray and pop in the oven for 10 minutes until smelling toasty and looking golden.

► Break up the chocolate and place it in the bowl along with the sugar, cream and butter. Set this over the pan and leave it for 5 minutes so it can melt without any encouragement – don't be tempted to stir it as this will make it go grainy.

► Allow the nuts to cool slightly and then roughly chop them. Add them to the chocolate and give it a good stir to make sure all the chunks have melted into a smooth sauce. Pour into the sterilised jars, or a bowl if you think it won't last more than a few days. Cool completely, so it is firm enough to spread.

► Store in the fridge for 2 weeks. Before serving, bring it to room temperature or just slather on really hot toast.

whipped blackberry soft cheese

This whipped soft cheese is heavenly slathered on to hot chewy bagels. The soft cheese melts a little and the fruit is gently warmed, giving it the sweetness that jam would otherwise add.

makes 300 g
100 g blackberries
2 tbsp caster sugar
½ tsp vanilla extract
  or vanilla bean paste
250 g full fat soft cheese

▸ Place the berries and sugar in a small saucepan over a low heat and stir gently until they begin to collapse and turn jammy. Turn off the heat and allow to cool completely. Once cool, add the vanilla.

▸ In a large mixing bowl, beat the soft cheese until light and fluffy. Once the berries are cool, fold these into the soft cheese so you have delicate swirls and pockets of fruit. Leave to set in the fridge. Serve at room temperature with toasted bagels.

pecan maple and lemon butter

When you have interesting flavoured bread for toasting, it is enough simply to butter it. But that doesn't mean the butter has to be plain old butter; you can spike it with an array of different tastes. I like the combination of lemon zest with maple syrup and some nuts thrown in for good measure, especially with a toast containing dried fruit, such as panettone or raisin bread.

makes 300 g

200 g unsalted butter, softened
125 g maple syrup
½ tsp finely grated lemon zest
25 g chopped pecans

▸ Place the butter in a large bowl and, using a hand-held electric whisk, beat it until pale and fluffy. Add half the maple syrup and beat in, followed by the lemon zest and then the rest of the maple syrup. Finally, fold in the nuts. Pack into a jar or bowl and cover. Refrigerate for up to 1 month. Remove from the fridge and spread on toasted panettone, crumpets or raisin bread.

orange blossom honey butter

You could just as well make this with any of the many flavoured honeys that are available. I like it on toasted malt bread or brioche. You can freeze any extra in greaseproof paper and use it on top of mince pies at Christmas, or to crown a stack of ricotta cheese pancakes.

makes 175 g
100 g unsalted butter, softened
75 g orange blossom honey
2–3 drops orange blossom water

▸ Place the butter in a large bowl and, using a hand-held electric whisk, beat it until pale and fluffy. Add half the honey and beat in, followed by the orange blossom water and then the rest of the honey.

▸ Once everything is smooth, pile on to a 25 cm square of greaseproof paper and roll into a long fat cigar shape. Twist the ends to seal and refrigerate for up to 3 weeks. Remove from the fridge and spread on a lightly toasted brioche.

gentleman's relish

This is my version of Elsenham's Gentleman's Relish, which is sold in small white pots that look like they belong in the bathroom, rather than the kitchen. John Osborn's original recipe for this anchovy spread, which was conceived way back in 1828, is a closely guarded secret. Use it to spread on toast that is ready to receive scrambled or poached eggs, char-grilled lamb or steak, or barbecued fish.

makes 100 g
8 anchovies in oil, drained
100 g unsalted butter
A pinch of ground ginger
A pinch of cayenne pepper
A pinch of grated nutmeg

▶ Place all the ingredients in a small saucepan and warm gently over a low heat until almost all of the butter has melted. Remove from the heat and stir until the last of the butter has melted. In that way you won't end up overheating the butter. Allow it to cool completely, stir well as it may have separated, and then pack into a small ramekin or clean jar. It will keep for a week.

rosemary, white beans, chorizo and rocket

Whizzing up cannelini beans is a bit like making houmous. They are quite bland in flavour, so they need lots of aromatics, such as garlic and rosemary. This spread is delicious on its own or with roasted tomatoes but hot spicy chorizo turns it into a real meal.

serves 2–4

100 ml extra virgin olive oil
1 garlic clove, peeled
1 sprig rosemary
400 g can cannelini beans
Juice of 1 lemon
4 x 2 cm-thick slices white bread
   or ciabatta
150 g chunky chorizo, sliced on
   the diagonal
A large handful of long-stemmed
   wild rocket
Salt and freshly ground
   black pepper

▸ Heat the olive oil in a small pan with the garlic and rosemary for a few minutes until bubbling, then turn off the heat and leave it to infuse.

▸ Drain the beans and rinse them under the tap. Shake them dry and tip into a food processor. Give them a brief whizz. Remove the rosemary from the oil and set aside. Tip the oil into the processor and whizz until you have a smooth purée. Add seasoning and lemon juice to taste.

▸ Preheat the grill. Place the slices of bread on a baking sheet and the chorizo on the same sheet, to one side. Grill for 2 minutes, turning over both the bread and sausage very carefully with tongs to crisp each side. Slather the toast with the bean purée and serve with the rocket and chorizo on top.

avocado, lime and black pepper

In the summer of most Antipodean climes, the avocado season means boxes of cheap flavoursome avocadoes. This is a favourite of one of my Australian friends. A good avocado is nutty and unctuous with a creaminess; it needs a dash of acidity to cut through the oil and some seasoning to tease out the natural flavours. You can add some chopped coriander, chopped tomatoes or crispy bacon if you tire of the combination below.

serves 4
4 slices granary bread
2 avocadoes
Juice of 1 lime
A few dashes of Tabasco sauce
Salt and freshly ground black pepper

► Toast the bread in the toaster until quite golden. Meanwhile, halve the avocadoes and remove the stones. I find the easiest way to do this is to place the avocado half on a chopping board and using an 18 cm chopping knife, chop down on the stone to stab it; it will get stuck to the blade and then you can bang the handle on the edge of a firm surface to release it.

► Using a dessert spoon, scoop out the flesh of the avocado from both sides and mash it up in a bowl with salt and pepper. Add the lime juice and enough Tabasco to taste. Spread it on to toast and serve.

creamed parmesan

The flavour of a good *Parmigiano Reggiano* cheese has many nuances from nutty and salty to honeyed and milky. This spread flaunts all of them. I like to spread it on a couple of toasted slices of ciabatta in place of butter and then clamp a rosy rare steak and some vivid green rocket in the middle. It's delicious just as it is on crostini (see page 21) with an aperitif, or topped with Parma ham, or even some steamed asparagus in season.

serves 4
75 g Parmesan, grated
2 tbsp white balsamic vinegar
4 tbsp extra virgin olive oil,
   plus extra for drizzling
1 ciabatta, cut into
   1–2 cm-thick slices
Salt and freshly ground
   black pepper

▸ Place the Parmesan in a food processor and blend with the balsamic vinegar. Then slowly trickle in the olive oil. Taste and season with black pepper, but add a touch of salt only if you can convince yourself it really needs it (remembering Parmesan is brined). Set aside at room temperature.

▸ Toast the bread under the grill until golden on both sides and spread with the Parmesan cream. Drizzle with a little extra virgin olive oil just to provide a glistening contrast against the pure colour of the Parmesan cream.

smoked mackerel pâté

Smoked mackerel has a wonderful oily, salty and smoky flavour, so it needs some equally punchy partners to stand up to it. Horseradish is perfect in this respect, but it needs a little crème fraîche and butter just to calm everything down. Serve with crackers, Melba Toast (see page 15) or with granary toast.

serves 6 as a starter
250 g smoked mackerel
    (about 3 fillets), skinned
2 small shallots, trimmed
    and roughly chopped
1 tbsp hot horseradish
Juice of 1 lemon
25 g unsalted butter, softened
100 g crème fraîche
Cayenne pepper, to taste
    and garnish

▸ Place the fish and shallots in a food processor and whizz until both are chopped up. Add the horseradish, lemon juice and butter, and whizz again until completely smooth. Stir in the crème fraîche.

▸ Taste for seasoning. It may need some cayenne pepper and a little more lemon juice. I'd be surprised if it needed any more salt. Once satisfied with the flavour, smear on to hot toast and dust with cayenne.

crostini with artichokes and parma ham

I like to go to the deli and get thicker than usual slices of Parma ham to adorn these crostini. The unusual flavour of artichokes is really hard to describe but it is this flavour that is tickled out by the lemon and the saltiness of the ham. Rye bread is a tricky one to toast as it is so dense, but that's what I love about using it for a change for crostini. It is really satisfying and has that malty tang that you don't get from white bread. You could use these flavours with the Canapé Crostini on page 21 to serve to guests at parties.

makes 8

200 g artichoke hearts in olive oil
50 g Parmesan, grated
30 g blanched almonds
Juice of ½ lemon
8 x 1.5 cm-thick slices rye bread
8 slices Parma ham
A handful of wild rocket
Extra virgin olive oil, to drizzle
Freshly ground black pepper

▸ Drain the artichokes from the oil, reserving the oil for later. Transfer the artichokes to a food processor and add the Parmesan, almonds, lemon juice and some black pepper. Whizz until you have a slightly textured paste, adding two to three tablespoons of the reserved oil to loosen the texture slightly. Set aside at room temperature while you make the crostini.

▸ Preheat the grill. Place the rye bread on a baking sheet and grill the bread for 2–3 minutes on each side until golden. Generously slather the artichoke paste over the toast, top with luscious folds of Parma ham and rocket and drizzle with a little more olive oil.

3

breakfast

Poached egg with chorizo
Gentlemen's relish and runny eggs
Spinach, black pudding and goats' cheese
Garlic roasted mushrooms with pancetta
Smoked salmon herb omelette
Challah French toast with bacon
Scrambled eggs
Bloody Mary spiked tomatoes
Poached Turkish eggs with dukkah

poached egg with chilli flakes, thyme and chorizo on toasted bread

Little chunky sausages of chorizo are packed with flavour and when fried they release all their paprikary juices. Another great thing about them is that they keep for ages, so this can become a good stand-by dinner.

serves 2

100 g chunky chorizo sausage, sliced thinly
½ tsp chilli flakes
1 tbsp thyme leaves, plus extra for garnish
4 eggs
4 slices white bread
Butter, for spreading

▸ Place a wide saucepan of water for the eggs on a high heat and bring to the boil. Meanwhile place the *chorizo*, chilli and thyme in a frying pan and slowly heat to crisp up the sausage, stirring occasionally so it cooks evenly. This should only take 2–3 minutes and when it starts to smoke, turn off the heat and let it sit in the pan to keep warm.

▸ Turn the heat down under the saucepan in which you are to cook your eggs. Break the eggs evenly around the edge of the saucepan and turn down the heat to a gentle simmer. Poach for 3 minutes, in barely simmering water – they should have glorious molten centres, but set whites.

▸ Meanwhile, pop the bread in the toaster and, when done, butter it and get it ready to receive the eggs on the plate. Fish each egg out and nestle on the toast. Heat the *chorizo* if you feel it could do with a final blast and spoon the *chorizo* and juices over the egg. Finally scatter with thyme leaves.

soldiers with gentleman's relish and runny eggs

This is my twist on the classic Victorian dish Scotch woodcock, which consists of Gentleman's Relish on toast smothered in scrambled eggs. It's become a bit of a joke to say someone can't boil an egg, but never was a truer word spoken in jest. Most people can't. My method is foolproof and keeps the whites creamy and yolks runny. You need to start off with room temperature eggs or the eggs will crack and will take longer to cook.

serves 2–4
4 large eggs at room temperature
4 slices white or brown bread
2 tbsp Gentleman's Relish
    (see page 36)

► To soft boil your eggs, place a medium saucepan of water on the hob and bring it to a rolling boil. Lower in four eggs and turn the heat down so they simmer gently for 1 minute. Turn off the heat completely, cover with a lid and set your timer for 4 minutes. Remove the eggs with a slotted spoon and place in egg cups. Don't allow them to sit for longer than a minute between pan and table as they will continue to cook.

► Meanwhile, toast your bread and slather it with the Gentleman's Relish. Cut into soldiers and serve with the eggs.

toast with spinach, black pudding and crumbled goats' cheese

This can be served as a hearty breakfast dish on a winter's morning or, if you want to serve just one toast per person, you could serve it as a tasty small starter for four people.

serves 2–4

225 g black pudding, sliced into 4
2 large tomatoes, sliced 1 cm thick
2 white English muffins, sliced in half
1 tbsp extra virgin olive oil
1 garlic clove, peeled and sliced
150 g spinach, washed
100 g goats' cheese, divided into 4
1 tsp clear honey
Salt and freshly ground black pepper

▸ Preheat the grill to high. Spread the black pudding and tomato slices on a baking sheet. Season the tomatoes with salt and pepper and then grill for 3–4 minutes. Turn over, add the muffins and cook for the same amount on the other side. Turn the muffins halfway through so they cook on both sides.

▸ Meanwhile, heat a frying pan or wok over a high heat. Add half the oil and garlic and half the spinach and, using a pair of tongs, toss it around so it cooks evenly, for about a minute, then tip into a mixing bowl. Cook the rest of the spinach in the same manner.

▸ Top the muffins with a couple of slices of the black pudding and tomato, and then a mound of spinach. Place on the same baking sheet and crumble over the goats' cheese and drizzle with honey. Slide back under the grill for 1–2 minutes so everything warms through and the cheese has melted and is flecked with golden bits.

garlic and oregano roasted mushrooms and pancetta on toasted sourdough

Big meaty mushrooms are best kept whole and roasted, so they retain all their juiciness and don't turn slimy as sliced mushrooms can. If you are vegetarian, leave out the pancetta, but think about replacing it with some shavings of Parmesan for a touch of saltiness.

serves 4
4 large or 8 medium field
    mushrooms, sliced
2 red onions, peeled and cut
    into wedges
2 garlic cloves, peeled and sliced
4 sprigs oregano, leaves only
100 g pancetta, cubed
2 tbsp extra virgin olive oil
4 slices sourdough bread
Butter, for spreading
Freshly ground black pepper

▶ Preheat the oven to 200°C/Gas 6. Place the mushrooms on a lightly oiled baking sheet. Tuck in the onion wedges around them. Scatter over the garlic, oregano and pancetta, drizzle with olive oil and season with black pepper. Roast for 25 minutes until the mushrooms and onions have softened.

▶ Pop the toast in the toaster, spread it with the butter and then pile the mushrooms, pancetta and onions on top.

smoked salmon thin herb omelette with sour cream on rye toast

These thin omelettes flecked with herbs and paprika are as simple and quick to make as pancakes. I sometimes roll them up with the filling and take them on picnics wrapped in greaseproof paper. My favourite, though, is to put them on toast and enjoy them for breakfast.

serves 4

4 eggs, beaten
1 tbsp chopped tarragon
3 tbsp chopped parsley
½ tsp paprika
100 ml sour cream
2 tbsp lemon juice
1 tsp Dijon mustard
25 g butter
4 slices rye bread
8 slices smoked salmon
50 g wild rocket
Salt and freshly ground
    black pepper

▶ Preheat the oven to 125°C/Gas 1. For the omelettes, beat together the eggs, tarragon, parsley and paprika with half a teaspoon of cold water in a mixing bowl, seasoning as you go. For the sour cream, mix together the sour cream, lemon juice and Dijon mustard in another bowl and set aside. Put a plate in the oven for keeping the omelettes warm.

▶ Heat about one teaspoon of the butter in a 12–15 cm frying pan over a high heat and swirl it around the pan. Add a quarter of the egg mixture, just enough to coat the base of the pan. Wait for 30 seconds, then flip over. Repeat with the remaining mixture, using the same amount of butter each time, so you have four omelettes, keeping them warm on the plate in the oven. When they are all ready, pop the toast in the toaster and butter using the remaining butter.

▶ Place a slice of salmon on each omelette, fold in half, so you have a semi-circle, add a second slice and fold again into a triangle. Place on the toast, drizzle with the sour cream and scatter with a few leaves of rocket.

challah french toast with bacon and maple syrup

Challah, the traditional braided Jewish bread, makes excellent French toast. With its high egg content it is the bread of choice in diners all over the States. Being really spongy and absorbent, it absorbs the egg and fries well without becoming soggy. You cannot beat the contrast of sweetness from the syrup and the saltiness of the bacon.

serves 2–4

3 large eggs, beaten
2 tbsp milk
A pinch of nutmeg
A pinch of cinnamon
4 x 2 cm-thick slices *challah*
8 rashers streaky bacon
25 g butter
2 tbsp vegetable oil
Maple syrup, to serve

▸ Preheat the grill to high. Mix together the eggs, milk and spices in a bowl. Put the *challah* slices into the eggs and milk and set aside for 5 minutes to soak up any remaining liquid.

▸ Place the bacon on a rack set over a baking sheet and grill for 3–4 minutes on each side until crisp.

▸ Meanwhile, heat the butter and oil in a wide frying pan over a medium heat. Add two slices of the soaked *challah* and cook for 1–2 minutes on each side until speckled with brown. Transfer to a plate under the shelf with the bacon in the grill, if you need to, to keep warm, while you fry your second batch. Serve 1–2 slices French toast per person along with the bacon and maple syrup.

scrambled eggs on toast

Scrambled eggs and the way they are cooked are a very personal thing. I like to use organic eggs for their flavour and also to know the hen has been happy when she has parted with her gift. I prefer them *baveuse*, the cook's term for runny or, if you want to be literal about the translation, from the French for 'dribbly'! I don't feel you need to add cream because if you cook them very slowly, they will be inherently creamy. This is not a 2-minutes task, but takes a good 8–10 minutes, so be a little patient, it's not that long to wait for your breakfast!

serves 2
5 large organic eggs
2 tbsp whole milk
15 g butter
4 slices white or wholegrain
  nutty bread
Butter, for spreading
Salt and freshly ground
  black pepper

▸ Crack the eggs into a mixing bowl. Beat the eggs together with the milk and seasoning. Meanwhile, heat the butter over a low heat in a heavy-based saucepan until melted. Add the eggs and leave to heat through, stirring occasionally for 2–3 minutes until they start to feel like they are thickening on the base of the pan. Turn the heat right down to its lowest setting and stir the base of the pan constantly for about 5 minutes to make sure they don't catch.

▸ Pop the toast in the toaster and, when done, get the slices ready on the plates and butter them. Take the eggs off the heat while they still look a little glossy, give them a final few stirs and divide on to the toast. Scatter with a little more cracked black pepper.

bloody mary spiked tomatoes on toast

These tomatoes are an effective hangover cure; arguably more so than the drink. There's no need to butter the toast as the buttery juices from the tomatoes will serve the same purpose. So don't worry about the amount of butter you are using to soften the onions; it is serving a dual purpose.

serves 4
50 g butter
2 red onions, peeled and sliced
1 red chilli, seeded and sliced
500 g cherry tomatoes
2 tsp vodka or red wine vinegar
½ tsp celery seeds or celery salt
1 tsp hot horseradish
A handful of coriander leaves
Salt and freshly ground black pepper
4 slices seeded brown bread

► Place the butter, onions and chilli in a large frying pan, cover and cook over a medium heat for 8–10 minutes until beginning to soften. Give them a stir every now and again. Add the tomatoes, vodka or vinegar, celery seeds and horseradish, cover and cook for a further 10 minutes, until the tomatoes begin to burst and lose their shape. Uncover and if the tomatoes are still juicy, simmer for 4–5 minutes to drive off the juices. Season to taste.

► Pop the toast in the toaster. Spoon the tomatoes on to the toast and scatter over the coriander.

poached turkish eggs
with dukkah

Poaching eggs is all about having very fresh eggs so the white coagulates.
If your eggs have been sitting around for a few days, then a capful of vinegar
in the water helps, but not too much or it leaves a metallic tang. *Dukkah* is an
Egyptian spice mix containing roasted nuts and seeds, which is traditionally
eaten with bread. Here, it works well as a seasoning in the butter.

serves 4

1 tsp coriander seeds
½ tsp cumin seeds
2 tsp sesame seeds
2 tbsp pine nuts
½ tsp chilli powder or
  cayenne pepper
50 g butter
200 g thick Greek yoghurt
1 small garlic clove, peeled
  and crushed
4 pitta breads
4 large eggs

▶ To make the *dukkah* butter, place the seeds,
nuts and chilli power or cayenne pepper in a
frying pan over a low to medium heat. After a
minute they should start to smell interesting,
so start stirring and make sure everything
toasts evenly for 4–5 minutes. Once they look
golden all over, remove from the heat and add
the butter, but don't heat it just yet.

▶ For the garlic yoghurt, mix together the
yoghurt and garlic in a bowl and set aside.

▶ Preheat the grill to high. Place a deep frying
pan over a high heat, fill up with water and bring
to the boil. Place the pitta breads on a baking
sheet and grill for 2 minutes on each side.

▶ Making sure the water is barely simmering,
break the eggs evenly around the edge of the
frying pan and leave them to sit for 3 minutes.
Use a timer if you can.

▶ Put the *dukkah* butter pan over a low heat.
Meanwhile, get four plates, remove the toast
from the grill and spread with the garlic yoghurt.
Grab a slotted spoon and lift out each egg and
sit on top of each yoghurty bread. Once the
butter is bubbling, pour it over the eggs.

veggie

Welsh rabbit
Bruschetta with tomatoes and basil
Bruschetta with mozzarella, olives and chilli
Bruschetta with broad beans
Caramelised shallots on soft cheese
Baked ricotta with tomatoes
Chilli aubergines with feta
Goats' cheese with tapenade
Indian scambled eggs on naan
Peppers and halloumi on pitta

welsh rabbit

So much more than just cheese on toast, Welsh rabbit has the piquancy of Worcestershire sauce and mustard to give it a tang. The splash of ale makes it more akin to fondue, which also mixes alcohol and cheese. Why is it called rabbit when it contains no meat, you might ask? Well, the name was conceived as an ironic slur on the Welsh; alluding to their poverty to imply they could not even afford one of the cheapest and most plentiful meats of the eighteenth century. The cheese is the poor man's rabbit. The recipe quite often goes by the name of rarebit as this makes it clearer that it contains no meat.

serves 2–4
4 slices wholegrain bread
250g mature Cheddar, grated
4 tbsp ale
½ tsp English mustard powder
½ tsp Worcestershire sauce

▸ Preheat the grill to high. Place the bread on a roasting tray and toast for 2 minutes on each side until golden.

▸ Meanwhile, place the cheese, ale, mustard and Worcestershire sauce in a small saucepan and put over a low heat. Stir gently until the cheese starts to melt and then keep going until everything is smooth. It might feel quite runny and separate slightly, but don't worry, it will right itself once it is grilled.

▸ Take the toast out from under the grill and transfer to a baking dish or baking sheet with sides. Pour the cheese sauce over the toast, so it covers the whole of the baking dish or sheet. Slide back under the grill for 2–3 minutes until lightly charred on top. Serve with a tomato and watercress salad.

veggie

bruschetta with tomatoes and basil

This is the sort of concoction that demonstrates how vital it is to use flavourful ingredients when the food is simple. The produce, not the chef, is the hero here. A simple tomato bruschetta relies on sweet, grassy smelling tomatoes, the kind that remind you they are soft fruit. A peppery olive oil and some sturdy bread help the proceedings too.

makes 8
6 ripe plum tomatoes, diced
4 tbsp extra virgin olive oil
8 basil leaves
8 slices country bread or *pain rustique*
2 garlic cloves, peeled and halved
Salt and freshly ground black pepper

► Place a griddle pan over a high flame or light a barbecue well in advance. Place the chopped tomatoes in a bowl and season them to tickle out their flavour. Douse them in half the olive oil, add the basil and toss through. Season again and set aside.

► Once the griddle pan is smoking hot, or the barbecue's coals are glowing an ashen grey, pop the bread on and toast for 2–3 minutes on each side until charred in places and crisp all over. Take off the heat and rub with the cut side of the garlic cloves.

► Spoon the tomatoes and their juices over the top and drizzle with the last dregs of olive oil. Eat immediately or they will become soggy.

bruschetta with buffalo mozzarella, olives, chilli and thyme

Soft milky buffalo mozzarella works wonders on top of a charred hunk of sourdough. The chilli, olives and lemon thyme give it a freshness and saltiness. Serve as a starter on a warm sunny day and buy the best mozzarella you can find. Look out for *burrata*, which is a fresh mozzarella with cream inside.

makes 4

250 g buffalo mozzarella
   or *burrata*, drained
50 g green olives, pitted
   and chopped
2 red chillies, seeded
   and roughly chopped
1 sprig lemon thyme
100 ml extra virgin olive oil
4 slices sourdough bread
1 garlic clove, cut in half

► Place a griddle pan over a high flame or light a barbecue well in advance. Rip up the mozzarella and put into a bowl along with the olives, chillies, lemon thyme and oil. Set aside for the flavours to mingle with each other while you make the bruschette.

► Once the griddle pan is smoking hot, or the barbecues coals are glowing an ashen grey, pop on the bread and toast for 2–3 minutes on each side until charred in places and crisp all over. Take off the heat and rub with the cut side of the garlic clove. Spoon the mozzarella, olives and chilli and all its oily juices over the bruschette. Serve with a pile of rocket on the side.

bruschetta with broad beans, pecorino and mint oil

I apologise upfront for suggesting you have time to burn by double-podding broad beans. But surely we all have someone in our life who is eager to please and we can palm this task on to. If not, it's worth making this early in the broad bean season so you can catch the beans before their green jackets get tough. If you have very young beans like this, you can skip the extra podding stage. If you prefer, you can use fresh or defrosted peas instead.

makes 12

7 tbsp extra virgin olive oil
1 sprig mint, leaves only, shredded
350 g podded broad beans or baby
    broad beans or peas
1 garlic clove, peeled
75 g pecorino, shavings or grated
    coarsely
Juice of ½ lemon
12 Olive Oil and Rosemary
    Bruschetta (see page 16)
Salt and freshly ground black pepper

▸ Place three tablespoons of the oil and all the mint in a jug, season and set aside. Heat a large saucepan of water until boiling. Tip the beans or peas into the pan and bring back to the boil. This should take roughly 3–4 minutes.

▸ Drain and run under cold water, before setting about the slightly laborious job of slipping the broad beans, if using, out of their dull green jackets. Discard the skins and place the beans or peas in a food processor with the garlic, half the cheese, all the lemon juice and the remaining olive oil. Blend until you have a chunky paste, season and taste, then season again if need be.

▸ Spread this on the bruschette and scatter with the remaining pecorino, drizzle everything with the mint oil and scatter over lots of black pepper.

sticky balsamic, caramelised shallots on soft cheese

Blanching shallots in boiling water makes easy work of peeling them and also part cooks them, so they need only be browned in the frying pan. This is a good starter to serve to people who don't eat meat, as it feels quite different from the usual veggie starters they get offered. If you can find banana shallots, which are meatier and easier to peel, try it with them, but blanch for a little longer until tender.

serves 4
500 g shallots, trimmed
25 g butter
2 tbsp extra virgin olive oil
2 tbsp caster sugar
4 tbsp balsamic vinegar
100 ml red wine
1 tbsp redcurrant jelly
4 slices rosemary foccacia
75 g full fat soft cheese

▸ Simmer the shallots in a pan of boiling water for 3–4 minutes to loosen their skins and soften them, then drain and set aside to cool. Once they have cooled, peel them.

▸ Heat half the butter and all the olive oil in a frying pan over a medium heat and cook the shallots for 10–15 minutes, until browned all over. Add the caster sugar and balsamic vinegar, let it bubble up and then add the red wine and let that cook for 2–3 minutes and reduce. Stir in the remaining butter and the redcurrant jelly. Take off the heat to cool a little as you want the shallots to be warm, not hot.

▸ Meanwhile, toast the bread in the toaster, spread with the soft cheese and pile the shallots over the top.

baked ricotta toasts with slow-roasted tomatoes

Slow-roasting tomatoes draws out their sweetness and makes their inherent flavour really intense. It might seem like a long time to wait for something on toast, but if you do a batch of tomatoes on a weekend, you can eat them in salads, sandwiches and quick suppers like this throughout the week. They don't need any attention while cooking and will keep for a week in the fridge.

serves 4

8 plum tomatoes, halved
2 garlic cloves, peeled and sliced
2 sprigs thyme
2 tbsp extra virgin olive oil
150 g ricotta
1 egg and 1 yolk
4 tbsp double cream
50 g grated Parmesan
4 squares of foccacia or ciabatta
A handful of basil, shredded,
   to garnish
Freshly ground black pepper,
   to garnish

► Preheat the oven to 150°C/Gas 2. Place the tomatoes, cut-side up, in a roasting pan and scatter with the garlic and thyme, then drizzle with the olive oil. Place in the oven and forget all about them for 1½ hours. By this time they should be dried out and concentrated.

► Take the tomatoes out of the oven and turn up the temperature to 200°C/Gas 6. In a small bowl, mix together the ricotta, egg and egg yolk, cream and Parmesan. Spread this mixture all over the bread. Place on a baking sheet and bake for 12–15 minutes until the ricotta has puffed up and becomes golden. Top with the tomatoes and scatter with basil and pepper.

veggie

roasted chilli and mint aubergines with feta on toasted pitta

Aubergine needs to be cooked carefully; too much and it becomes a soggy pulp, and too little, it is a bit like chewing kitchen paper. Slicing the aubergine and then grilling it gives it a crunchy exterior and a creamy inside and then once dressed in all the punchy flavours of the Levant, it truly comes to life.

serves 4

2 aubergines, sliced into 2 cm-
   thick rounds
6 tbsp extra virgin olive oil
2 red chillies, seeded and chopped
A handful of mint, finely chopped
1 garlic clove, peeled and crushed
Juice of 1 lemon
200 g feta, crumbled
Salt and freshly ground black pepper
4 pitta bread, to serve

▶ Preheat the grill to high. Place the aubergine slices on a flat baking sheet and brush with four tablespoons of the olive oil on both sides. Season them well with salt and pepper and grill for 8–10 minutes on each side.

▶ Meanwhile, make the dressing by mixing together the rest of the oil with the chillies, mint, garlic and lemon juice in a large bowl that is big enough for you to add the aubergines to once they are cooked. Season to taste, remembering you are going to add some salty feta later on.

▶ When the aubergines are nicely charred and soft all the way through, tip them into the dressing and stir to combine. Set aside while you toast the pitta. Heat a griddle until very hot and add the pitta. Cook, pressing down on them to ensure you get good dark lines, for 2 minutes, then flip them over and cook for a further 2 minutes on the other side. Pile on to toasted pitta breads and crumble the feta over the top.

grilled goats' cheese with tapenade toast and beetroot

Small toasts of melted goats' cheese are the very essence of French bistro food. I like to slather my baguette slices with tapenade before grilling them, which I might make, as below, or buy from a deli if I see one that looks glossy and delicious. The walnut dressing and beetroot make me feel a little bit more nourished or at least fool me into thinking this is healthy food.

serves 4

For the tapenade
150 g black olives, pitted
½ garlic clove, peeled
A handful of flatleaf parsley,
    roughly chopped
1 sprig rosemary
3 anchovies
100 ml extra virgin olive oil

For the toast topping
½ small baguette, sliced on
    the diagonal into 4 slices
2 x 100 g goats' cheese
60 ml extra virgin olive oil
2 tbsp walnut oil
1 tsp Dijon mustard
Juice of ½ lemon
100 g mixed baby leaves
3 cooked beetroot, chopped
Salt and freshly ground
    black pepper

▶ To make the tapenade, place the olives and garlic in a food processor and blend until chopped. Add the parsley; remove the needles from the rosemary and discard the stalk, then add that too. Blend until finely chopped. Add the anchovies and two tablespoons of the oil and blend until you have a rough paste. Add a little more oil and continue to blend, then add the rest, blending until you have a sludgy paste.

▶ Preheat the grill to high. Place the bread on a baking sheet and grill one side for 1–2 minutes until golden. Remove from the oven and spread the untoasted side with the tapenade. Slice each goats' cheese in half and divide between four slices of the bread. Place the tray under the grill to melt the cheese; it should take 2–3 minutes to bubble up and become golden.

▶ Meanwhile, place the oils, mustard and lemon juice in a mixing bowl, whisk to emulsify and season. Add the leaves and beetroot and toss gently so they are coated in dressing.

▶ Divide the salad into individual bowls. Once the cheese has melted, pile one plain and one cheesy toast on to every mound of salad.

veggie

indian scrambled eggs on toasted naan bread

Somewhat surprisingly, eggs lend themselves really well to the heat and aromas of spices and chilli. This may not be everyone's cup of tea in the morning, but it makes a great quick supper, or a mid-morning brunch dish. I love these stand-by dishes that you can cook without having to venture to the shops, as you usually have most of the ingredients in the cupboard and naan breads freeze well. It is not the most beautiful dish, but is one of the most addictive.

serves 2

40 g butter
1 large onion, peeled and sliced
½ tsp salt
A pinch of turmeric
1 tsp cumin seeds
2 naan breads
1 garlic clove, peeled and crushed
2 red chillies, seeded and chopped
1 tomato, seeded and chopped
6 eggs, beaten
4 sprigs coriander, to garnish

► Preheat the grill. Heat half the butter in a saucepan and add the onion, salt, turmeric and cumin. Cover with a lid, turn the heat to low and cook for 10 minutes until really soft. Meanwhile, place the naan breads on a baking sheet, brush with the remaining butter and place under the grill until toasted.

► Make sure your onions are not catching on the bottom of the saucepan, but if they are, give them a stir. Add the garlic and chillies and stir for 5 minutes more until slightly caramelised. Add the tomato and eggs and stir briskly until the eggs thicken. Serve as soon as they set with a sprig of coriander.

peppers and halloumi on toasted pitta with capers and lime dressing

I love the combination of sweet, silky peppers and squeaky, salty halloumi cheese. The capers and lime are both quite sharp and acidic so they perk everything up. This is my idea of a perfect everyday, nothing special, but oh-so-delicious summer lunch.

serves 4
Garlic and Thyme Pitta Toasts
  (see page 20)
3 red peppers, halved and seeded
3 tbsp extra virgin olive oil
Juice of 2 limes
2 tbsp capers, rinsed
2 red chillies, seeded and chopped
A handful of flatleaf parsley,
  roughly chopped
250 g halloumi cheese, drained
  and sliced
Extra virgin olive oil, for brushing
Freshly ground black pepper

▶ First make the pitta toasts as described on page 20.

▶ Preheat the grill to high. Place the peppers, cut-side down, on a baking sheet and slide under the grill for 10 minutes until the skins are charred and the flesh has softened slightly. Remove from the grill and transfer to a bowl and cover with cling film; this will help loosen the skin, while keeping all the precious juices.

▶ Meanwhile, make the dressing. Whisk together the olive oil and lime juice and then add the capers and chillies and pour in any juices released from the peppers.

▶ Grab a large mixing bowl and put the flatleaf parsley in there. Peel the skin off the peppers, slice the flesh and add to the parsley.

▶ Heat a griddle pan over a high heat. Brush the halloumi cheese with oil and fry for 2 minutes on each side until golden. Tip the halloumi into the bowl with the other ingredients and give it all a good stir. Season with black pepper, then pile on to the pitta toasts and serve.

veggie

75

fish

Mackerel, watercress and cherry tomatoes
Haddock, mustard and cheese
Omelette with prawns and chilli
Tiger prawns and feta
Prawn and sesame toasts
Salmon and herb salad toasts

mackerel with watercress and roasted cherry tomatoes

This is really delicious if you cook the mackerel on a barbecue. You could char the toast on the side and then simply pile it on top. As you can't always rely on the weather for a barbecue, here is a fail-safe, all-weather alternative.

serves 2–4

Juice of 1 orange
Juice of 1 lemon
1 tsp cumin seeds
1 garlic clove, peeled and crushed
1 tbsp *harissa* paste
2 tbsp extra virgin olive oil
4 mackerel fillets, skin on
300 g cherry tomatoes
1 baguette, cut in half lengthwise
    and then into 15 cm pieces
50 g watercress
Lemon wedges, to serve

▸ Preheat the grill to high. Mix the orange and lemon juices, cumin, garlic, *harissa* and olive oil in a small bowl and add the mackerel fillets and tomatoes. Stir gently to coat.

▸ Place the mackerel fillets, skin-side up, on a lightly oiled baking sheet and scatter the tomatoes around. Cook for 3–4 minutes until almost cooked through, then flip over and cook for a minute on the other side.

▸ Take out of the oven and slide the bread on another baking sheet, under the grill for 1–2 minutes until toasted on one side, pile on the watercress, top with the mackerel and tomatoes and serve with lemon wedges.

smoked haddock, mustard and cheese rarebit

No one seems very sure about how Welsh rabbit morphed into 'Welsh rarebit', but the consensus seems to be that if the cheese is joined by other ingredients, such as buck rarebit, with an egg, the rabbit disappears, thus becoming a rarebit. Smoked haddock and cheese make an unctuous combination, which is quite a hearty snack and can easily become supper. This is the sort of dish I like to rustle up after a long cold walk, before starting a fire and settling in for the evening.

serves 4–6
300 ml whole milk
350 g smoked haddock fillet,
   skinned (undyed if possible)
60 g unsalted butter
60 g plain flour
75 g mature Cheddar, grated
1 tsp English mustard
Juice ½ lemon
2 egg yolks
6 slices granary bread
Freshly ground black pepper

▸ Place the milk in a deep frying pan and bring to the boil. Turn the heat to very low and lower in your haddock. Poach very gently for 5–6 minutes until it is cooked through.

▸ Meanwhile, melt the butter in a small saucepan and add the flour. Stir together over a medium heat. Lift the haddock from the frying pan on to a plate and then strain the milk into the saucepan a little at a time until you have a smooth sauce. Simmer for a further 3–4 minutes to bring to the boil then remove from the heat.

▸ Preheat the grill to high. Put the cheese and mustard into the white sauce and stir until melted, then beat in the lemon juice and egg yolks. Remove the skin from the haddock, discard any bones and flake into the sauce.

▸ Pop the bread on to a baking sheet and toast on both sides under the grill until golden. Transfer to plates, then pile the fish mixture on to the toast, spreading it right over the edges to protect the crusts. Return to the grill and grill for 3–4 minutes until golden and puffed up. Serve with freshly ground black pepper.

omelette with prawns, coriander and chilli on toast

This is not a typical omelette, more of an open-faced omelette with all my favourite stir-fry flavours thrown in. Like many omelettes, it was born out of one of those moments when you have odds and ends in the fridge and get creative. I have remade it and drizzled it with a little oyster sauce, which works in a similar way to a bit of trashy ketchup on a bacon and egg butty. Feel free to join in my guilty secret, but here it is without the oyster sauce.

serves 4

6 eggs

1 tbsp chopped coriander

Finely grated zest of 1
   unwaxed lemon

20 g unsalted butter, plus extra
   for spreading

100 g tiger prawns

2 mild red chillies, finely chopped
   (seeded if you don't trust them)

6 spring onions, trimmed and
   sliced thinly or shredded

4 slices ciabatta

Salt and freshly ground
   black pepper

▶ Preheat the oven to 220°C/Gas 7. Beat the eggs in a mixing bowl, add the coriander and lemon zest and plenty of seasoning. Heat the butter over a high heat in a 15 cm frying pan (one that can be transferred to the oven, so no plastic parts). Pour the eggs on top and let them sizzle and get some colour on the underside.

▶ Add the tiger prawns and half of both the chillies and spring onion and start to draw the edges into the middle so the uncooked egg runs to the edges. Just before everything is cooked, place in the oven for 3–4 minutes to cook the top and puff up.

▶ Put the ciabatta in the toaster. Open the oven door and make sure you use an oven cloth to remove the omelette, as you will be tempted to grab the docile-looking hot handle, which is not a good idea. Cut the omelette into four wedges, butter your toast and serve each wedge on the toast. Scatter with the remaining spring onions and chillies and serve.

tiger prawns and feta on toast

Although some people are horrified by the fusion of fish and cheese, especially the Italians who balk at the tourists who ask for Parmesan on their *linguine vongole*, sweet plump prawns go brilliantly with salty feta. I like to serve this on thick slices of granary toast, so the garlicky, buttery juices infused with the aniseed tang of fennel soak in and become irresistibly soggy.

serves 2

4 tbsp extra virgin olive oil
2 garlic cloves, peeled and halved
1 celery stick, finely sliced
1 tsp fennel seeds
225 g tiger prawns, peeled
Juice of 1 lemon,
100 g feta, crumbled
4 x 1.5 cm-thick slices
   granary bread

► Heat half the oil in a large frying pan over a high heat and add the garlic, celery and fennel and fry for 2 minutes. Then add the prawns and fry for a further 2–3 minutes until they turn pink. Tip out into a mixing bowl and squeeze over the lemon juice. Crumble in the feta and give everything a good mix.

► Toast the bread in the toaster, divide equally between two plates and spoon the prawns and spinach over the top.

prawn and sesame toasts with sweet chilli dip

Everyone has fallen for the charms of prawn toasts in Chinese restaurants, but here is a version that is respectable enough to serve at parties. Thai cooks make theirs with pork, which adds a little fat and flavour to the lean prawns, helps them stick together and makes them a little more economical to cook in large numbers. If you don't want to cook them all, you can spread the paste on the bread and freeze for another time.

makes 45

1 baguette, sliced 1 cm thick
2 spring onions, trimmed
  and roughly chopped
150 g peeled prawns
300 g minced pork
1 egg
1 tbsp fish sauce
1 tbsp finely chopped
  coriander stalks
1 tsp sesame oil
600–900 ml sunflower or
  vegetable oil for frying
20 g sesame seeds
Sweet chilli sauce, to serve

▸ Preheat the oven to 150°C/Gas 2. Pop the bread on a baking sheet and into the oven for 5–8 minutes to dry out slightly; this will stop it absorbing oil like a sponge!

▸ Meanwhile, place the spring onions in a food processor and blend until they are finely chopped. Add the remaining ingredients, except the sesame seeds, and blend until combined.

▸ Take the bread out of the oven. Spread the paste on each baguette slice, scatter with sesame seeds and lightly press these on to the paste.

▸ Heat the oil in a wok or deep fat fryer to 190°C. This is when a cube of bread browns in 30 seconds. Have ready a baking sheet covered with kitchen towel. Fry the toasts in batches of four at a time for 2–3 minute, paste-side down, and then for 2 minutes, paste-side up, until golden all over. Fish them out gently with a slotted spoon and drain on the kitchen paper, then transfer to the oven, while you cook the rest. Serve with sweet chilli dipping sauce.

fish

85

salmon and herb salad toasts

The toasted pitta in this salad works in the same way as it does in the Middle Eastern salad *fattoush*. It adds a hot crunch to counter the cool of the radish and cucumber. All these textures set off the soft mix of herbs and smoky fish. Sumac is a bright red berry that is ground and added as a tangy seasoning to Middle Eastern dishes. Use a little more lime if you can't find it.

serves 4

3 pitta breads
3 tbsp extra virgin olive oil
160 g hot smoked salmon fillets
10 radishes, thinly sliced
½ cucumber, thinly sliced
3 spring onions, trimmed and
  thinly sliced on the diagonal
A handful of coriander leaves
A handful of flatleaf parsley leaves
A handful of mint leaves
Juice of 1 lime
½ tsp sumac

▸ Preheat the grill. Split the pitta breads in half so they are only one layer and place on a baking sheet. Brush with oil and grill for 2–3 minutes on each side until crisp and golden. Cool slightly then tear into small pieces.

▸ Flake the hot smoked salmon into a large mixing bowl. Add the sliced radishes, cucumber, spring onions and herbs. Give everything a good toss. Drizzle over the remaining olive oil and squeeze over the lime. Add the torn pitta, toss everything once again, divide on to four plates and scatter each one with a pinch of sumac.

6

poultry

Chicken and fennel-roasted mushroom
Chicken livers, sage and pancetta
Avocado toasted tortillas
Duck with cherries and Madeira

griddled chicken with lemon and fennel-roasted mushroom and aïoli on toasted ciabatta

This is one of my all-time favourite open sandwiches, which I have been cooking ever since I worked in Tom Conran's eponymous café. Everyone I have served it to loves the aniseed tang of the fennel against the juicy chicken and mushroom and layer of garlicky mayonnaise.

serves 4

2 x 225 g chicken breasts, halved

4 field mushrooms, stalks trimmed off

2 red onions, peeled and cut into wedges

2 tbsp extra virgin olive oil, plus extra for drizzling

2 garlic cloves, peeled and sliced

1 tsp fennel seeds

Zest and 1 tbsp juice of 1 unwaxed lemon

2 tbsp thick Greek yoghurt

4 ciabatta rolls, halved

25 g baby salad leaves

Freshly ground black pepper

▸ Place each chicken breast half individually in a polythene bag and bash out with a rolling pin until 2 cm thick. Heat the griddle over a high heat until smoking. Add the chicken and tuck the mushrooms and onion wedges around them.

▸ Drizzle with olive oil and season with freshly ground black pepper. Cook for 5 minutes, then flip everything over. Scatter over the garlic, fennel and half the lemon zest and continue to cook for a further 4–5 minutes until the chicken is cooked through and the vegetables have softened.

▸ In the meantime, mix together the yoghurt, two tablespoons of olive oil, lemon juice and the remaining zest and set aside.

▸ Have a bowl ready and take off the vegetables from the griddle as they are ready. Remove the chicken when that is ready and add the ciabatta rolls, cut-side down, for 1 minute to toast lightly. Transfer to serving plates, spread the toast with the yoghurt mixture, pile on the baby leaves and serve the chicken, mushrooms and onions on top.

chicken livers, sage and *pancetta* on toasted sourdough

Livers are very quick to prepare; they need to be swiftly browned over a high heat without becoming overcooked, which is when they take on a bitter flavour. This is quite a rich dish, so if you are serving it as a starter, you will only need one piece of toast per person, but for supper you might need two.

serves 2–4
4 slices sourdough bread
50 g butter
1 red onion, peeled and sliced
75 g *pancetta*, cubed
1 garlic clove, peeled and crushed
400 g chicken livers, cleaned
1 tbsp plain flour
8–10 sage leaves
100 ml balsamic vinegar
Salt and freshly ground
    black pepper

▸ Preheat the grill and place the sourdough slices on a baking sheet. Heat one-third of the butter in a frying pan over a low heat and cook the onion and *pancetta* for 5–8 minutes until the latter is opaque and the former is really soft and translucent. Add the garlic for a further minute. Tip both the onion and *pancetta* on to a plate while you brown the chicken livers.

▸ Add the same amount of butter and wait just a moment for it to get really hot again. Toss the chicken livers in the flour and add to the pan along with the sage so they really sizzle. Season all over and toss them around for 2–3 minutes until browned but pink on the inside.

▸ Slide the sourdough on a baking sheet under the grill. Pour the balsamic vinegar into the pan and let it bubble up. Return the onions and *pancetta* to the pan. Warm through for a minute or two, checking the liver is just cooked. Take off the heat and stir in the remaining butter to thicken. Transfer the toast on to plates and then drape over the chicken livers.

chicken and avocado toasted tortillas

This is the kind of snack that is good to make when you have a movie to watch and want to curl up on the sofa in your comfy clothes. You can vary the fillings, adding borlotti beans instead of chicken, but don't leave out the cheese, as you need this to make it stick together.

serves 2–4
2 cooked chicken breasts, shredded
4 spring onions, trimmed and
    thinly sliced
1 avocado, stoned (see page 39),
    peeled and chopped
2 tomatoes, seeded and roughly
    chopped
2 tbsp chopped coriander
Juice of 1 lime
100 g Cheddar, grated
4 flour tortillas
Extra virgin olive oil, for brushing
Sour cream, to serve
Salt and freshly ground
    black pepper

▸ Mix together the chicken, spring onions, avocado, tomatoes, coriander and lime in a bowl. Season and scatter with cheese. Lay two tortillas flat on a chopping board and brush with oil, then flip over so the oil is on the underneath. Spread the mixture all over them. Top with the other tortillas and press down slightly, then brush lightly with oil.

▸ Heat a ridged griddle pan over a high heat until really hot. Transfer one of the tortillas to the griddle, oil-side down. Cook for 1–2 minutes until toasted, pressing gently with the back of a large fish slice to help the cheese stick the whole thing together.

▸ Lift the tortilla off the griddle using the fish slice and flip over. Do this quickly because if you hesitate, it will collapse. Cook on the other side for 2 minutes and then lift off the plate and leave for 1 minute. Cook the other tortilla in exactly the same way. Slice into wedges and serve with the sour cream.

seared duck with dried cherries and madeira on toasted brioche

Browning and then deglazing duck in this classical way doesn't quite seem to fit with most people's expectations of a supper on toast. However, the meaty, buttery, deglazed juices are sublime on top of light toasted brioche.

serves 4

50 g dried sour cherries
120 ml Madeira wine
40 g salted butter
2 x 200g duck breasts, skinned
4 small brioches, halved
1 garlic clove, peeled and sliced
1 tsp orange zest
2 tbsp curly parsley, chopped
Salt and freshly ground
   black pepper

▶ Place the cherries in a small bowl and pour over the Madeira wine. Allow them to soak for 15 minutes to plump up. Meanwhile, place a griddle pan on a high heat ready for the brioche. Place a frying pan over a high heat for the duck.

▶ Add half the butter to the frying pan and wait a minute for it to stop foaming and get hot. Add the duck and season with salt while in the pan. Cook for about 4 minutes, then flip over and cook on the other side for 2–3 minutes so it is still rosy inside. Remove the pan from the heat and rest the duck on a board.

▶ Place the cut side of the brioches on the griddle for 1 minute until golden – they will turn quite quickly as they are high in butter, so watch them carefully.

▶ Meanwhile, return the pan you used for the duck to the heat and add the garlic. Stir for 30 seconds until lightly golden then pour in the Madeira and cherries and the orange zest. Allow this to bubble up and reduce slightly. Then take off the heat and stir in the remaining butter.

▶ Slice the duck and divide the brioches on to plates. Top with the duck, spoon over the juices and scatter with parsley.

poultry

7

meat

Peppered lamb with salsa verde
Sausage and taleggio bruschetta
Steak, rocket and anchovy butter
Merguez sausages with red onions
Ham croque monsieur
Porchetta and apple mayonnaise
Baked beans with pork belly

peppered lamb with salsa verde and watercress on toasted baguette

Lamb neck is surprisingly tender, but it can be fatty so it needs to be cooked over a high heat to crisp up any fattiness. The sharp, punchy salsa verde cuts through the richness. A lean pork fillet or white fish will work in place of the lamb neck if you would like to ring the changes occasionally.

serves 4

350 g lamb neck fillets
160 ml extra virgin olive oil
1 tbsp mixed peppercorns, crushed
Finely grated zest and juice of 1
   unwaxed lemon
A large handful of flatleaf parsley,
   stalks removed
1 garlic clove, peeled
A handful of mint leaves
2 anchovies, drained
25g capers, rinsed
1 baguette
A large handful of rocket
Salt and freshly ground
   black pepper

▶ Preheat the oven to 180°C/Gas 4. Smother the lamb with two tablespoons of the oil. Mix the peppercorns and lemon zest on a plate and roll the lamb in them until evenly coated. Transfer to a roasting tin, slide into the oven and cook for 20–25 minutes until just cooked through. If in doubt, cut it in half through the centre; it should be moist but not too rosy.

▶ Meanwhile, make the salsa verde. Place the parsley in a food processor with the garlic, mint and a small pinch of salt. Process until finely chopped. Add the anchovies, capers and four tablespoons of the oil and blend again. Add another four tablespoons of the oil and blend until you have a vibrant green sauce. Season with pepper and a squeeze of lemon juice.

▶ Cut the baguette in half then slice it horizontally in half again. Place on a baking sheet. When the lamb is ready, take it out and let it rest for 5 minutes. Turn the grill to high and toast the bread on the cut side for 3–4 minutes. Slice the lamb thinly. Divide the rocket between the baguettes and drizzle with the remaining oil and a squeeze of lemon. Top with the lamb, drizzling with a little salsa verde.

sausage and taleggio bruschetta

This is a very quick snack, which really hits the spot. If you can, look out for Italian sausages called *lucanica*, which are sometimes flavoured with fennel. You need a sausage that is full of tasty meat and a good proportion of fat to soak into the bread, so try not to buy anything full of rusk, which is a filler in cheap sausages.

makes 4

2 Italian sausages, skinned
1 tsp fennel seeds
½ tsp chilli flakes
1 tsp lemon zest
150 g taleggio cheese, rind removed and roughly cubed
4 x 2cm-thick slices rustic bread
Freshly ground black pepper

► Preheat the grill to high. Mix together the sausage meat, fennel seeds, chilli, lemon zest and some black pepper in a bowl, then gently stir in the cubes of cheese.

► Place the bread on a baking sheet and toast on one side. Flip over the bread and spread with the sausage and cheese mixture, right to the edges to protect the crusts from burning. Return to the baking sheet, slide under the grill and toast until the sausage is cooked and the cheese melted and bubbling.

griddled steaks with rocket and anchovy butter

The saltiness of anchovies goes remarkably well with steak and is not as overpowering as you might imagine. If you're not a fan of anchovies, try making the butter with wholegrain mustard and lemon zest instead. If you're not used to cooking steak you need to get a feel for it. A fellow cook told me you could compare the feel of a cooked steak to different parts of your face to gauge whether it is rare or medium: touching a rare steak feels as if you're touching your cheek while medium is comparable to the chin. I think this is quite a good way, but you may want to do it with clean hands!

Serves 4

2 x 300 g sirloin steaks

1 tbsp extra virgin olive oil, plus extra to drizzle

4 slices black olive ciabatta or bread

30 g unsalted butter, softened

2 tbsp anchovy paste

Zest of 1 unwaxed lemon and juice of ½ of it

A large handful of wild rocket

Salt and freshly ground black pepper

▶ Heat a griddle pan over a high heat until really hot. Brush the steaks with oil, season the tops and place, oiled- and seasoned-side down, on the griddle. Cook for 3–5 minutes, depending on their thickness. Season the other side, flip the steaks over and cook for another 2–4 minutes. They should feel a bit like the flesh on your chin, and no longer like the flesh on your cheeks which should give you a rosy interior without being bloody; remember they'll cook further after resting. Take off the heat and let the steaks rest on a board. Trim off any large pieces of fat.

▶ Add the ciabatta slices to the griddle and let them toast and soak up any juices left by the steaks. This should take 3 minutes on each side. Meanwhile, place the butter in a bowl and beat in the anchovy paste and lemon zest.

▶ Once the ciabatta slices are golden, spread with the anchovy butter. Slice the steaks and divide between the toasts. Top with rocket and give everything a drizzle of olive oil and a squeeze of lemon.

merguez sausages with red onions and capers on toasted ciabatta

Cooking sausages in this *'agradolce'*, or sweet and sour way, is very Sicilian; it cuts right through their fat. I like it with lamb sausages, such as the North African merguez sausages which are so popular in the South of France, but you could use venison for a change or just an ordinary pork banger.

serves 4
3 tbsp extra virgin olive oil
8 merguez lamb sausages
2 red onions, peeled and sliced
2 sprigs rosemary
1 tbsp sugar
2 tbsp sherry vinegar
2 tbsp capers
2 plum tomatoes, quartered
4 slices foccacia
2 dried chillies
Freshly ground black pepper

▸ Heat a frying pan with the oil over a medium heat. Add the lamb sausages and brown for 3–4 minutes, add the onions, break up the rosemary and scatter that on top. Sprinkle over the sugar. Fry over a medium heat, tossing the pan occasionally for 10 minutes until the sausages are golden.

▸ Add the sherry vinegar, capers, tomatoes, chillies and a splash of water to stop everything from drying out and continue to cook with the lid on for a further 10 minutes until the sausages are cooked through, and the onions are soft.

▸ Preheat a griddle. Toast the bread for 1–2 minutes on each side. Serve two sausages on each slice of bread and drizzle over the onions and sauce and other good things left in the pan, discarding the chillies as you come across them. Grind over some black pepper.

classic gruyère and ham croque monsieur

Ham and cheese: it's a marriage made in culinary heaven. The croque monsieur is a Parisian creation: smoky slices of ham with a sumptuous, oozing béchamel sauce laced with tangy mustard and Gruyère. Eat it hot, in all its molten glory.

serves 2
40 g butter, softened
4 x 2 cm-thick slices white bread
1 level tbsp plain flour
6 tbsp whole milk
1 egg yolk
2 tsp Dijon mustard
75 g Gruyère, grated
4 thick slices ham

▸ Preheat the grill. Butter two slices of bread using about one-third of the butter and place on a chopping board with the buttery sides facing down. Melt the remaining butter in a small saucepan over a medium heat and add the flour. Stir them together until they are blended, then add the milk gradually until the mixture has become smooth and very thick. Remove from the heat and stir in the egg yolk, mustard and grated Gruyère, then beat the sauce until the cheese has melted.

▸ Spread half this mixture over the unbuttered sides of the two slices of bread. Place two slices of ham on top of each and sandwich with the other unbuttered bread slices. Press them down lightly. Flip over the 'sandwiches' using a palette knife so they are buttered-side up, place on to a baking sheet, and grill for 2 minutes until golden. Remove from the oven and flip over once again. Pour over the remaining sauce – it is quite thick – and slide back under the grill for 2 minutes until bubbling and golden and delicious. Cut into diagonal halves and serve immediately.

slow-roasted *porchetta*, rocket and apple mayonnaise

Don't go to the trouble of slow roasting a joint of pork solely for this recipe, but plan a dinner of meltingly tender pork one night so that you can have a fabulous lunch the next day. If using all the pork for sandwiches, you'll be able to make about eight; four if you're having a respectable dinner as well.

serves 4–8

1 onion, peeled and finely chopped
4 garlic cloves, peeled and chopped
4 bay leaves, finely chopped
1 sprig rosemary, finely chopped
2 tsp salt
½ tsp whole cloves
1 tbsp fennel seeds
Zest of 1 unwaxed lemon
1 tsp chilli flakes
1.6 kg pork shoulder or leg, boned
   and opened flat with rind scored
1 tbsp extra virgin olive oil
1 ciabatta loaf
2 tbsp apple sauce
100 ml mayonnaise
A large handful of wild rocket
   or mustard leaf

▶ Preheat the oven to 150°C/Gas 2. Place the onion, garlic, bay leaves, rosemary and one teaspoon of the salt in the food processor and blend until finely chopped. Add the cloves and half the fennel seeds, along with all the lemon and chilli and blend for 10 seconds to combine.

▶ On a board, open out the pork, skin-side down, so it is flat. Smear the mixture over the middle then roll up tightly and tie with string. Place in a roasting tin. Dry the skin with kitchen paper then smear the oil and remaining salt over it. Scatter over the remaining fennel seeds. Place in the oven for 2½ hours. After this time, the flesh should be yielding to a fork, so turn up the temperature to 200°C/Gas 6 for 25–30 minutes to work on making that crackling blister. If it stubbornly refuses, stick it under the grill for a minute or two until it complies.

▶ Slice the ciabatta horizontally and then vertically into four slices. Heat a griddle pan and toast the ciabatta slices, cut-side down, for 3–4 minutes until charred. Leave the other side soft.

▶ Swirl the apple sauce into the mayonnaise and drape over the ciabatta. Tear apart the meat and keep aside some crackling. Divide the meat, rocket and crackling between each portion.

baked beans with pork belly

This is a great one-pot dish to cook for a party as you can cook it in advance. The pork belly becomes so tender it will flake under the pressure of a fork and the sauce is sweet and smoky. Also, it gets better the next day and can be left on a buffet without spoiling. It might seem unthinkable that you could entertain with beans on toast, but serve it along with a basket full of different types of toast wrapped in a linen cloth and a plate of salted Normandy butter and it becomes quite elegant.

serves 4–6

2 tbsp vegetable oil
400 g pork belly, rind and bones removed and cut into 3 cm cubes
2 red onions, peeled and sliced
1 red pepper, seeded and finely chopped
½ tsp paprika
½ tsp English mustard powder
2 garlic cloves, peeled and crushed
400 g *passata*
250 ml boiling water
2 tbsp cider vinegar
3 tbsp molasses or dark muscovado sugar
2 x 400 g cans haricot beans or cannelini or borlotti beans
8 slices sourdough or granary bread
Salted butter, for spreading
Salt and freshly ground black pepper

▸ Heat the oil in a large casserole dish and brown the slices of pork belly until it gets a little bit of colour on all sides. Add the onions, pepper and spices. Turn down the heat to low and cook for 10 minutes with the lid on, stirring occasionally until soft.

▸ Add the garlic, *passata*, water and vinegar and season with a good pinch of salt and freshly ground black pepper. Cover with a lid and simmer for 1 hour. After this time, check that the pork belly is beginning to tenderise; it should eventually collapse under the pressure of a fork.

▸ Give everything a good stir, add the sugar and one teaspoon of salt and taste to check the seasoning. Add the beans and if it looks a little dry, add a splash of boiling water. Cover and return to the hob for a further 30 minutes and then uncover for 20–30 minutes more, until you have a thickened sauce.

▸ Allow the flavours to settle for 15 minutes, while you make some toast. Butter the toast and place it on plates. Spoon over the beans and serve.

meat

107

8

sweet things

Toasted banana bread
Pain perdu with passion fruit
Bostock almond toasts
Torrijas
Stem ginger nectarines
Chocolate and peanut butter toastie
Raisin toast with lime mascarpone
Balsamic figs and goats' cheese

toasted banana bread

Banana bread is the kind of bread you can make when you have never stepped into a kitchen. The ingredients just need to be mixed together, poured into the right sized tin and left to do their magic in the oven. This bread is designed to be toasted and buttered, or spread with ricotta, so it is not as cakey as some banana bread recipes. The only secret here is to use the ripest, blackest bananas you can. Save some in the freezer when you find them ripening past their eating best.

makes 1 loaf
200 g self-raising flour
125 g soft light brown sugar
1 tsp ground cinnamon
½ tsp ground nutmeg
A pinch of salt
50 g butter, melted
1 egg, beaten
60 ml whole milk
2 ripe bananas (about 250 g),
    peeled and mashed
Butter or ricotta, to serve
Blueberry jam, to serve

▶ Preheat the oven to 180°C/Gas 4. Grease a 900 g loaf tin (14 x 21 cm) and line the base with non-stick baking parchment.

▶ Measure out the flour and sugar and add the spices and salt. Mix together the melted butter, egg, milk and mashed banana and tip into the dry ingredients. Lightly stir to combine, so there are no floury pockets left, but don't fret about any lumps, which are fine. Spoon into the loaf tin using a spatula to scrape out every last drop.

▶ Bake on the middle shelf for 30–35 minutes. Test with a skewer in the centre: it should come out clean when ready. Allow to cool in the cake tin for 10 minutes. Turn out on a wire rack, if you have one, or a plate and set aside to cool completely. Slice and toast and serve with butter or ricotta and blueberry jam.

amaretto pain perdu
with passionfruit syrup

Pain perdu is simply an elegant way of saying eggy bread or French toast.
It seems to validate it being served as a pudding, which is just fine by me,
as I adore it. Adding some amaretto to the egg gives it an elegant twist
and using a buttery, already egg-enriched brioche makes it very light
and thoroughly decadent.

serves 4
3 eggs, beaten
2 tbsp double cream
2 tbsp amaretto
3 tbsp caster sugar
A pinch of ground nutmeg
4 x 2 cm-thick slices brioche
4 passionfruit
4 tbsp sunflower oil
15 g butter
Strawberries, to decorate

► Preheat the oven to 200°C/Gas 6. Whisk the
eggs with the cream, amaretto, one tablespoon
of the sugar and nutmeg in a wide bowl. Dip
both sides of the brioche slices in the egg
mixture and set aside to soak up its goodness.

► Meanwhile, make the syrup. Cut the passionfruit in half and extract as much of the pulp
as possible. Pass the pulp through a sieve into
a saucepan and add the sugar and 100 ml of
cold water. Turn the heat on and leave low
until the sugar has dissolved and the mixture
is syrupy enough to coat the back of a spoon.
Set aside.

► Take a large frying pan and add half the oil
and butter. Place over a medium heat and wait
until the sizzling stops. Add as many pieces
of brioche as you can and fry for 2–3 minutes,
then flip over and fry for a further 2 minutes
until crisp. Transfer to a baking sheet and
place in the oven to keep warm and to puff
up slightly, while you cook the rest.

► Just before serving, reheat the passionfruit syrup. Serve two slices of *pain perdu*
on each plate with some syrup drizzled
over and a few strawberries, to decorate.

sweet things

111

bostock almond toasts

This is a clever way to use up stale brioche, which is not known for its keeping qualities and tends to dry out quickly. Essentially, the recipe is a frangipane (a mixture of ground almonds, eggs and butter), which is spread on day-old brioche that has lost its appeal as a buttery soft treat and needs a little assistance.

makes 8

150 g unsalted butter, softened
150 g caster sugar
1 egg and 1 yolk
150 g ground almonds
½ tsp orange flower water
8 x 3 cm-thick slices stale brioche
75 g flaked almonds

▸ Preheat the oven to 190°C/Gas 5. Line a baking sheet with non-stick parchment paper.

▸ Place the butter and sugar in a bowl and, using a hand-held electric whisk, beat together until light and fluffy. Beat in the eggs, almonds and orange flower water. Spread this mixture over the brioche slices right up to the edges and then scatter the top with the flaked almonds.

▸ Place each one on the baking sheet and bake for 8–10 minutes, until the brioche is toasted and the topping is puffed up and tinged with brown. Serve hot or cold with coffee in the morning.

torrijas

While you can now find *torrijas* all over Spain at any time of the year, they were initially only an Easter treat. They were the first indulgence after the abstinence of Lent. The method of soaking the bread in milk and then dipping it in egg makes the end result really sweet and soggy. The sweetness from the sherry and the cinnamon spike it with a real warmth.

serves 4

200 ml whole milk
2 tbsp caster sugar
1 orange with 2 strips of orange
 peel removed
1 baguette, a day old, cut into
 2 cm-thick slices
5 tbsp sweet sherry
3 eggs, beaten
½ tsp ground cinnamon
2 clementines
40 g Spanish marcona almonds,
 roughly chopped and toasted
100 g clear honey
25 g unsalted butter
2 tbsp sunflower oil

▶ Heat the milk in a small pan with the sugar and orange peel until the sugar has dissolved.

▶ Meanwhile, find a large shallow dish where you can spread out the bread in one layer. Add two tablespoons of the sherry to the milk and remove the orange peel. Pour the warm milk over the bread and set aside for 15 minutes to soak up the milk and become really soft.

▶ Meanwhile, in a separate bowl, beat the eggs and add the cinnamon. Rinse out the milk pan so you can use it for the sauce.

▶ To prepare the honey and orange sauce, peel off the skin and pith of the clementines and slice them into rounds. Catch any juice in your saucepan and add the almonds, honey and the remaining three tablespoons of sherry. Simmer for 5 minutes until the nuts are warm and then remove from the heat.

▶ Heat the butter and oil in a frying pan over a medium heat. Dip the bread into the egg and fry in the pan for 2–3 minutes until golden. Transfer to a clean plate and cover with foil while you cook the rest. Add the clementine slices to the honey sauce. Serve two *torrijas* per person and spoon over the honey and clementines.

stem ginger nectarines on toasted panettone with ice cream

This dish offers a real sensation of temperatures as well as tastes. The hot nectarines are spiked with warming ginger and the crunchy panettone is spiced with cinnamon and nutmeg, whereas the ice cream is teeth shatteringly cold and sweet. A wonderful combination, which makes a great quick pudding.

serves 4

4 nectarines, stoned and halved
2 tbsp soft brown sugar
2 tbsp chopped stem ginger
25 g salted butter
100 ml Marsala wine
4 slices panettone
Vanilla or stem ginger ice cream, to serve

► Preheat the oven to 200°C/Gas 6. Place the nectarines in a shallow ovenproof dish and scatter over the sugar, stem ginger, butter and wine. Cover with foil and bake for 15 minutes until the nectarines are soft. Take off the foil and bake for a further 5 minutes until slightly caramelised.

► Meanwhile, heat a griddle pan and toast the panettone slices, cut-side down, for 3–4 minutes until marked with lines. Divide the panettone between four bowls with a scoop of ice cream and serve with two halves of nectarine and some of the delicious pan juices.

chocolate and peanut butter toastie

If you have ever tasted Reese's peanut butter cups, then you will know the magical combination of chocolate and peanut butter. The contrast of sweetness and saltiness sends your mouth into a frenzy. I like to make this with any remains of my Chocolate Hazelnut Spread (see page 30), but you can just as easily buy the chocolate spread.

serves 4
4 x 1 cm-thick slices white bread
30 g unsalted butter, melted
2 tbsp chocolate spread (shop bought or see page 30)
3 tbsp crunchy peanut butter
1 tbsp golden caster sugar, to serve

▸ Place the slices of bread on a chopping board. Brush each one with butter, then flip the slices over so they are butter side down. Spread two slices with the chocolate spread and spread the other two slices with the peanut butter. Sandwich together the two slices so the chocolate bread stays put and the peanut butter bread flips over on top of them, butter side uppermost. Press down at the edges to make sure nothing is escaping.

▸ Heat a ridged griddle pan over a medium heat and fry the bread for 2 minutes, until golden. Flip over and fry for another 2 minutes. Then take off the heat and, using a fish slice, transfer the sandwiches to a board. Let them sit for 2 minutes and then cut in half. While warm, scatter with golden caster sugar for some texture on the outside.

sweeet things

117

raisin toast with lime mascarpone, mango and honey

Perfumed mangoes are wonderful when they are in season, especially the Alfonso variety, and this is a good quick way to use them up. The lime juice brings out their fragrance and the honey helps rebalance the sweetness. I love to serve this on a sweet toasted bread streaked with plump raisins, but malt loaf or a slice of ginger cake lightly toasted also works wonders.

serves 2–4

125 g mascarpone cheese
Zest of 1 lime
4 slices raisin bread
½ mango, peeled and stoned
2 tbsp clear honey

► Beat together the mascarpone and lime zest. Toast the raisin bread in the toaster or on a griddle until lightly charred. Spread with the mascarpone, top with the mango and drizzle with honey.

sticky balsamic figs and goats' cheese on walnut toast

This is a dish that has one foot in the cheese camp and another in the pudding course. If you manage to find fig balsamic vinegar, then that is just perfect for this; otherwise an aged balsamic will do. Only make this when figs are ripening on the trees into their much-loved honeyed sweetness, or their flavour will be bland. Choose thin-skinned figs, the black-skinned figs tend to be the best.

serves 4

4 black figs
2 tbsp light muscovado sugar
50 ml balsamic or fig balsamic vinegar
150 g soft goats' cheese
25 g icing sugar
4 slices walnut bread

▶ Preheat the oven to 190°C/Gas 5. Place the figs on a chopping board and cut a cross in each one, only half way through. Place cut-side up in a shallow baking dish. Scatter over the sugar and drizzle over the balsamic vinegar. Place in the oven for 15 minutes until the figs are soft and slightly caramelised.

▶ Meanwhile, heat a ridged griddle pan on the hob until really hot. While waiting for this to reach temperature, beat the goats' cheese with the icing sugar in a bowl. Place the bread on the griddle and press down on top so it scores the bread with dark lines. Turn over and griddle on the other side for a further few minutes. Spread with the goats' cheese and top with the sticky figs.

index

1 3 5 7 9 10 8 6 4 2

This edition published for The Book People Ltd, Hall Wood Avenue, Haydock, St Helens, WA11 9UL

Published in 2009 by Ebury Press, an imprint of Ebury Publishing

A Random House Group Company

The Random House Group Limited Reg. No. 954009

Addresses for companies within the Random House Group can be found at
www.randomhouse.co.uk

A CIP catalogue record for this book is available from the British Library

The Random House Group Limited supports The Forest Stewardship Council (FSC),
the leading international forest certification organisation. All our titles that are printed
on Greenpeace approved FSC certified paper carry the FSC logo. Our paper procurement
policy can be found at www.rbooks.co.uk/environment

To buy books by your favourite authors and register for offers visit www.rbooks.co.uk

Printed and bound in China by C & C Offset

ISBN 9780091928308

Design: Smith & Gilmour
Photography: William Reavell
Food styling: Tonia George
Prop styling: Tabitha Hawkins